HOW YOU CAN GET
THE MOST OUT OF LIFE
AT ANY AGE . . .

Free
SPIRIT

. . . AND HOW IT MIGHT
MAKE YOU A MILLIONAIRE

Al Neuharth is the author of these other books:

- ◆ Plain Talk Across the USA

- ◆ Profiles of Power

- ◆ Truly One Nation

- ◆ Window on the World

- ◆ World Power Up Close

- ◆ Nearly One World

- ◆ Confessions of an S.O.B.
  (national best seller)

Hᴏᴡ ʏᴏᴜ ᴄᴀɴ ɢᴇᴛ
ᴛʜᴇ ᴍᴏsᴛ ᴏᴜᴛ ᴏғ ʟɪғᴇ
ᴀᴛ ᴀɴʏ ᴀɢᴇ ...

Free SPIRIT

... ᴀɴᴅ ʜᴏᴡ ɪᴛ ᴍɪɢʜᴛ
ᴍᴀᴋᴇ ʏᴏᴜ ᴀ ᴍɪʟʟɪᴏɴᴀɪʀᴇ

Al Neuharth

To Marly
Dream! Dare! Do!
Al Neuharth

NEWSEUM
BOOKS

Published by Newseum Books. The Newseum is a museum of
news created and funded by The Freedom Forum, Inc.,
1101 Wilson Boulevard, Arlington, Virginia 22209.

All proceeds from the sale of this book accrue to the Newseum.

ISBN 0-9655091-8-4
Printed in the United States of America
November 2000

Second Printing
July 2003

To Free Spirits
of all ages
and all races
all over the world

PROLOGUE

Free Spirit defined ...

So you're not sure exactly what "free spirit" is? Or whether you want to be one? You're not alone.

When we founded The Freedom Forum in 1991, we wanted a slogan or credo for that international foundation, which is dedicated to fostering freedoms for all people. A study committee suggested:

Free Press. Free Speech. Free Spirit.

I loved it. But some of our key associates balked at the "free spirit" part. Here's why:

For some, it still was a queasy euphemism for the doings of "oddballs." It conjured up images of people like Forrest Gump, or the town crackpot, or the school misfit.

In the olden days, people would say in hushed tones of disapproval, "They're kind of free spirits, you know."

Not so much anymore, and certainly not for me.

In my book, free spirits dream, dare and do. A free spirit can be a risk-taker, a visionary, an innovative leader, an entrepreneur, or a courageous achiever who accomplishes great things beyond his or her normal circumstances.

Free spirit is individualism. Original thinking. Saying no to the status quo. Looking for better ways to learn and to live. To succeed and to share.

Free spirit makes freedoms work

Free spirit is what makes all of our First Amendment freedoms work. Free press. Free speech. Freedom of religion. Freedom to assemble. Freedom to petition.

Benjamin Franklin and his fellow declarers of the Declaration of Independence had free spirit. So did Paul Revere and the Minutemen. Thomas Jefferson and the other framers of the Constitution.

Sitting Bull and his Native American Indians had it when they fought Lt. Col. George Custer in the Battle of the Little Bighorn. Civil rights pioneer Rosa Parks had it when she refused to move to the back of the bus. The Rev. Martin Luther King Jr. had it when he dreamed his way to the mountaintop. Susan B. Anthony had it when she founded the women's rights movement. My associates had it when they reinvented the newspaper at USA TODAY. Bill Gates had it when he founded Microsoft.

Free spirit has created everything from better mousetraps to new nations.

If you are a free spirit, or a wannabe, this book can help you get the most out of life at any age.

Free Spirit rewarded ...

Free spirit is something people often talk about. Generally respect. But rarely honor.

The Freedom Forum has been honoring people and organizations it considers free spirits since 1992.

Former hostage and journalist Terry Anderson was the first recipient of The Freedom Forum Free Spirit Award. He received $100 for every day he was held captive in Lebanon. His take: $245,500.

Also honored over the years were big shots and big names like former first lady Barbara Bush, and small shots like Keen Umbehr, a trash collector from Alma, Kansas.

In all, 39 individuals were honored. Cash awards ranged from $10,000 to $245,500.

Million-dollar ante

The annual Al Neuharth Free Spirit of the Year Award, successor to that previous long-standing honor, ups the ante considerably. It carries with it up to $1 million from the sponsoring Freedom Forum. The award is given annually to a person in the news who has stirred the public's hearts and souls by demonstrating the human capacity to dream, dare and do.

So far, six people, all news-makers such as Burmese democracy advocate Aung San Suu Kyi and blind mountain climber Erik Weihenmayer, have received the Al Neuharth Free Spirit Award. Their take: $250,000 to $1 million.

The Associated Press

Aung San Suu Kyi

More details about the award are in the Epilogue, page 99.

You don't have to be a big shot to become an award winner — just a free spirit.

TABLE OF CONTENTS

FREE SPIRITS I HAVE KNOWN

CHAPTER 1

HOW TO SAY "NO" TO THE STATUS QUO

All progress has resulted from people

who took unpopular positions. "

— Adlai E. Stevenson, 1954

Our nearly 3-year-old Andre says "no" a dozen or more times a day. Examples:
- No, I don't want to take a nap.
- No, I don't want to get out of the swimming pool.
- No, I don't want to eat my broccoli.

No! No! No!

Our 4-year-old Karina asks "why" over and over daily. Like:
- Why can't I watch 10 more minutes of Nickelodeon?
- Why is God making it rain when I want to go outside?
- Why won't Alexis (her 9-year-old sister) let me in her room?
- Why can't I take Eevee (her Maltese puppy)

along to school, or to church, or to the grocery store?

Why? Why? Why?

The "nos" and the "whys" that come out of the mouths of babes are their ways of challenging the status quo.

Parents need to respond thoughtfully to children's nos and whys. Never "just because I say so!" Never with another no. But

The Freedom Forum/Scott Maclay

"Why aren't there any girls' heads on the mountain?" daughter Karina asked her dad during a Neuharth family trip to Mount Rushmore.

with a reason or an explanation. Or, maybe even a change in the rules, reforming the family status quo.

No, or why, are as important in the vocabulary of grown-ups as in that of kids, although adults might use them somewhat less frequently and a bit more reflectively.

As adults, we should never be satisfied with things as they are. Life is either an ongoing challenge, or it is nothing.

In my professional life, each sunrise has sparked new adventures. In my personal life, I made the mistake of forgetting that at age 65. Vowed then that I would never marry again, let alone have more children.

But a very pretty and peppy woman I met on the beach in Florida changed all that. Rachel Fornes and I were married when I was 68. She was 26 years younger.

She taught me how to live and love again. Now we are blessed with six adopted children, ages 8 months to 9 years.

They guarantee that there is no such thing as the status quo at our home. That home is a very children-friendly overgrown log cabin that takes all the hard knocks kids can deliver.

The quo has lost its status

Actually, there is no longer any status quo — or as Webster calls it, "existing state of affairs" — anywhere in the world.

That's really not new. Just more so now. The world has become a huge global village. Just as Canada's Marshall McLuhan predicted almost 40 years ago it would. One village, linked electronically, with instant and constant global communications. Thanks mostly to the satellite and the Internet.

Now, people everywhere see more, hear more, know more, do more, go more. That makes us want to change more.

Change things at home. At school. At work. Change the way we look at race. Or religion. Or sex.

Change how we use the Web. Or what we watch on TV. Or listen to on the radio. Or read in our newspapers.

That change in newspaper reading really started in the 1970s. The company I headed, Gannett, then owned 78 dailies across the USA. But circulation at many was declining, as it was for most newspapers everywhere.

I asked Lou Harris, then the foremost national pollster, to find out why. After extensive and expensive research, his answers boiled down to these:

◆ The television generation is not going to read dull, gray newspapers.

◆ It wants a maximum of information with a minimum of time and hassle.

That, more than any other factor, caused us to start USA TODAY in 1982. We made it look like TV in print. Lots of color. Big photos and graphics. Shorter stories, but lots of them.

McPaper's McNuggets

Our competitors and critics quickly and sarcastically labeled USA TODAY "McPaper." But within a few months or years, most of them were stealing our McNuggets.

For some, it took longer to change. The venerable Great Gray Lady, *The New York Times*, didn't introduce color until 1997.

Change scares some people of all ages.

In the long-running best seller, "Who Moved My Cheese?" two little mice called "Sniff" and "Scurry" taught two people named "Hem" and "Haw" about the inevitability of changing, or starving to death.

The "haves" of the world, especially members of "the establishment," are most resistant to change. They fear losing some of what they have. Mostly they want to hang on to these two treasures:

◆ Security
◆ Superiority

"Have nots" generally, but not always, seek or welcome change.

Change should translate into improvements for

all, near term or long term.

Those who are on the cutting edge of change ultimately will be winners, even though the road may be rocky along the way. Those who resist change will become losers, even though their path temporarily may seem smoother.

PLAIN TALK

Free spirits rock the boat but stay afloat.

Wilma Mankiller

When I met Wilma Mankiller, I popped the obvious question: "How did you get your name?" Her quick quip: "I earned it!"

Actually, "Mankiller" is a Cherokee military title that means someone who watches over the villages. And she has. Mankiller became the first female head of a major tribe when she was elected Cherokee chief in 1985.

Chief Wilma Mankiller at a Cherokee powwow.

By challenging Native American status quo, she not only has strengthened Cherokee Nation sovereignty and treaty rights but also has become a visible and viable national force for gender and racial equality.

When Wilma Mankiller says "no" to the status quo, men and women of all races and ages listen. Her free spirit helps them join in a constructive "yes."

The Freedom Forum/Scott Maclay

Carl Rowan with Project Excellence scholars.

Carl Rowan

Carl Rowan and I met 50 years ago. He had recently arrived in Minneapolis as the *Tribune's* first newsroom black staffer. I was an Associated Press reporter in Sioux Falls, South Dakota, attending media meetings in the Twin Cities.

"Al," he said, "I'm a poor black country kid from Tennessee and you're a poor white country kid from South Dakota. We're both gonna shake things up!"

He sure did, for a half century. As a reporter, syndicated columnist, TV commentator and ambassador. But at his death September 23, 2000, his Project Excellence, which in 13 years offered $92 million in college scholarships to black high school achievers in the Washington, D.C., area, may have been his most free-spirited achievement.

He often talked, sometimes with tears in his eyes, about how he changed the status quo for those high schoolers by making it "cool" to be smart.

FREE SPIRIT

CHAPTER 2

HOW TO DEVELOP A THICK SKIN, BUT KEEP AN OPEN MIND

> *Let me never fall into the vulgar*
>
> *mistake of dreaming that I am persecuted*
>
> *whenever I am contradicted.* "
>
> — Ralph Waldo Emerson, 1838

If you challenge the status quo, you might as well paint a bull's-eye on your chest. The darts and arrows will come at you.

Not just from your enemies, but even from some friends. Not only from competitors, but often from co-workers. Sometimes even from family.

If you develop a thick skin, most of that stuff will bounce off. But if you also keep an open mind, some of it will sink in, as it should.

Most thin-skinned people have trouble separating scoldings or insults, which generally are destructive, from constructive criticism.

I've had my share of insults in bucking the establishment or the established. But I've also been the target of criticism that really turned out to be constructive. Examples of both:

◆ When we started USA TODAY, Ben Bradlee,

Neuharth and former *Washington Post* Executive Editor Ben Bradlee enjoy a laugh at a Freedom Forum media conference in St. Petersburg, Russia.

then executive editor of *The Washington Post*, was asked if he thought the new kid on the block was a "good newspaper."

His contemptuous response: "If it is, then I'm in the wrong business."

◆ Linda Ellerbee, erstwhile critic on TV, was asked what she thought about the fact that USA TODAY's color ink didn't rub off on your hands.

Ellerbee quipped: "It [USA TODAY] doesn't rub off on your hands or on your mind."

Bradlee's remark was a meaningless insult. So

we laughed it off by joking with each other that "Ben finally has admitted he is in the wrong business."

Actually, the frequent public and critical exchanges between Bradlee and me were mostly attention-getting acts as far as I was concerned. Later, after his retirement from the *Post* and my "retirement" from USA TODAY, we appeared together at media conferences as far away as Russia and laughed at and with each other.

Ellerbee's criticism turned out to be constructive, albeit she didn't intend it to be. She helped us realize that some of our early issues were a bit soft or fluffy. Over time, we added more substance, without losing the colorful style.

An ego under control

When our Freedom Forum began plans for its $50 million Newseum, the world's only interactive museum of news, early whispered reactions were that it would just be an ego-satisfying monument to Neuharth.

We picked up on that. When we lured USA TODAY editor Peter Prichard to join us to direct establishing and running the new Newseum, we agreed that we would absolutely avoid overplaying any reference to me, USA TODAY or Gannett.

Result: When the Newseum opened in 1997, it

got universally complimentary reviews, from the press as well as the public.

When we announced plans in 2000 to enlarge and move the Newseum from Arlington, Virginia, to the prestigious Pennsylvania Avenue and 6th Street location between the Capitol and the White House, *The Washington Post* ran a strong editorial endorsement of the move, welcoming us to town.

Scolding and spanking

Unintended destructive criticism often comes from family or loved ones.

Many, or most, parents are guilty of simply scolding their kids when they misbehave, rather than offering helpful advice. Scolding is almost as bad as a spanking, which should be strictly verboten.

Our Ariana, nearly 3, is in motion all the time and into her share of mischief. When that borders on the serious side, I'll usually tell her as calmly as possible "I'm disappointed you did that" and explain what she should, or should not, have done.

Then I'll ask her, "Why do you think I told you that?" Her smiling answer invariably is, "Because you love me!"

 PLAIN TALK

Free spirits
laugh at
criticism
but learn
from it.

Ted Turner

Two years before the media elite disparaged USA TODAY as "McPaper," the fast-food of journalism, they had branded Ted Turner's fledgling CNN the "Chicken Noodle Network." Ted

The Associated Press/CNN

Satellites opened the door to Ted Turner's CNN in 1980.

wouldn't let the naysayers nix a good idea. He laughed at them.

It was that spunk and similarity that led me to propose a corporate marriage in 1985: Gannett and Turner Broadcasting. We came so close that Ted introduced me to a friend as his "new boss." But when I couldn't guarantee him he'd eventually get the top title succeeding me in the combined company, he bowed out.

The same tough skin that steeled "Captain Outrageous" in winning America's Cup has confounded his critics in the media, business and political world.

George Steinbrenner during a cold, but winning, October playoff game in 1999.

The Associated Press/Matt York

George Steinbrenner

George Steinbrenner can handle heat. And in the Big Apple, where he mainly holds forth with his Yankees, who are universally loved or hated, that means hot heat.

So having been a Yankees fan all my life, I quickly became a Steinbrenner fan when he visited our Florida home, Pumpkin Center, in early 1980.

USA TODAY was just a gleam in my eye. I told him about it. He laughed and said I was nuts to think a national newspaper could succeed. Told me later that on the way home he thought, "They ought to put Neuharth in a straitjacket."

Since USA TODAY's success, Steinbrenner tells that story often. That's "The Boss." He can take heat or dish it out. And laugh about it either way.

CHAPTER 3

HOW TO
TAKE
RISKS
THAT
REAP
REWARDS

Two roads diverged in a wood, and I —

I took the one less traveled by,

and that has made all the difference."

— Robert Frost, 1916

L ife is a game and a gamble. The road to every reward is strewn with risks. One key to getting the most out of life is to figure out how to take risks that lead to the rewards you are seeking. Those rewards may, or may not, be financial. Maybe just fulfillment. In these most important areas:

♦ Personally
♦ Professionally
♦ Spiritually
♦ Socially

Many of those who gambled their careers with us when we started USA TODAY did so because their old job was no longer fun or challenging. Many were women or minorities whose sex or skin color blocked their advancement where they were. For many, their risk-taking paid off big time. Two prime examples:

- ◆ Cathie Black, who became the first female publisher of USA TODAY in 1984.
- ◆ Karen Jurgensen, who became the first female editor of USA TODAY in 1999.

Jurgensen was assistant city editor at *The Miami News* when we started USA TODAY. She gave up her security there, piled herself, her 5-year-old daughter, Kirsten, and their belongings in her 1977 Ford Granada and drove from Miami to Washington, D.C.

She started as topics editor for the Life section at USA TODAY. Earned her way up the ladder and now as the editor calls the shots on everything that goes into the largest newspaper in the USA.

Black had made her reputation on Madison Avenue. Was publisher of *New York* magazine, but her path seemed blocked in the huge Rupert Murdoch empire.

She joined USA TODAY as president in 1983, became publisher the next year.

After I left active management at USA TODAY, she moved onward. Black now heads the huge Hearst magazine empire, including such titles as

Cosmopolitan and *Esquire*.

Black's departure opened the way for a former young "whiz kid," who helped plan USA TODAY, to become its publisher. Tom Curley, then a 30-year-old promising newsman, was one of those who left a secure job and

Neuharth and USA TODAY Publisher Cathie Black check out a copy in the pressroom.

spent more than a year doing research and planning for a possible new newspaper. He went on to other training and development jobs in Gannett. Became USA TODAY president in 1986 and publisher in 1991.

In addition to hiring more women and minorities at Gannett, we found other ways to help.

When I met Bob and Nancy Maynard, they had

Bob and Nancy Maynard in *The Oakland Tribune* newsroom.

quit prestigious and well-paying jobs at *The Washington Post* and *The New York Times,* respectively, to pursue a dream. On a shoestring, they developed a respected institute in the San Francisco Bay Area to train minority journalists.

They were natural choices as a team to run *The Oakland Tribune* when Gannett acquired it. Four years later, when FCC regulations caused us to relinquish *Tribune* ownership to try to buy a major Bay Area TV station, we sold the *Tribune* to the Maynards at a bargain price.

They became the first African Americans to own a metropolitan U.S. daily.

Black, Curley, Jurgensen and the Maynards all gambled and won.

Salami, cheese and poker

I learned about gambling at age 14. Worked as a "butcher boy" in an old-fashioned meat market in the tiny prairie town of Alpena, South Dakota, part time while in high school. A happy-go-lucky Welshman named Tom Rosser, who owned and ran the one-man shop, paid me $1 a week and all the salami and cheese I could eat.

More importantly, he taught me how to play poker. During slow times — and there were many in that little market — we played poker. The betting limit was one penny. Some weeks I won or lost 50 cents or more.

I learned these early lessons about gambling and life:

- You must skillfully play whatever cards you are dealt.
- Take chances and have fun.

- A little bluffing sometimes makes you a winner.
- Don't be afraid to risk everything you can afford to lose.

Later, in the big outside world, I found that no-risk managements run no-fun and ultimately no-win businesses.

PLAIN TALK

Free spirits
travel the
byways
as well
as the
highways.

Gloria Steinem

Gloria Steinem was a bra-burning feminist when I asked her to keynote a meeting of the nearly all-male New York State Newspaper Publishers Association in 1970. "These guys are chauvinists," I told her, "so lay it on the line."

Gloria Steinem touts her *Ms.* magazine in 1977.

She did. With the same candor and can-do spirit that made her risk her professional reputation with *Ms.* magazine. It quickly became, and still is, an outspoken voice for women's rights.

Steinem, who once said, "Women's total instinct for gambling has been satisfied by marriage," rolled those dice in September 2000. At age 66, she said "no" to her personal status quo. Took marriage vows in the Oklahoma home of old pal Wilma Mankiller to be a lifetime "partner" with David Bale.

Korczak and Ruth Ziolkowski

Korczak and Ruth Ziolkowski in 1981 with "Crazy Horse" mountain in background.
Inset: Crazy Horse sculpture.

Robb DeWall/Crazy Horse Memorial

When Korczak Ziolkowski started blasting away in South Dakota's Black Hills in 1948, I was a skeptical summer intern at the *Rapid City Journal.* His vision: Turn a mountain into a huge sculpture of Chief Crazy Horse.

Korczak is dead. I've changed from a Crazy Horse skeptic to a big booster. His spirit and his monumental project live on as wife Ruth and other family members chip away at the mountain.

They are fulfilling Korczak's promise to Lakota Chief Standing Bear, who wanted "the white man to know that the red man has great heroes, too."

In Dakota, Korczak risked his reputation as a renowned sculptor from New England. Today, as the carvings that will be much bigger than nearby Mount Rushmore draw 1 million awed visitors a year, his risk is paying off.

FREE SPIRIT

CHAPTER 4

HOW TO FIND THE LIGHT AT THE END OF THE TUNNEL

I hope we never live to see the day when a thing is as bad as some of our newspapers make it. "

— Will Rogers, 1934

Many readers and viewers think the media print and air too much negative or bad news. Often they're right.

Watergate spawned a generation of cynics in journalism schools on college and university campuses across the USA.

Carl Bernstein and Bob Woodward of *The Washington Post* were properly acclaimed for their excellent investigative journalism, which brought about President Richard Nixon's resignation.

Dirt under every carpet

Many young wannabe journalists decided the best way to fame and fortune was to emulate Woodward and Bernstein. Result: They were determined to find dirt under every carpet in front of every politician's or business person's door, whether it was there or not.

Fortunately, many in that generation of cynics have now become more responsible as newspaper and TV news editors. Importantly, most journalism graduates now coming off campus have re-established the traditional "who, what, when, where and why" of journalism.

From my perspective, most of us fall into one of these categories, professionally or personally:

- ◆ Cynics
- ◆ Skeptics
- ◆ Optimists

Cynics seek the worst in everything and everybody. Skeptics are guarded and inquisitive, but open-minded. Optimists believe there is light at the end of every tunnel.

At home, cynics in the family are grumpy at the breakfast table and not happy about the new day's tasks. Skeptics eat their food rather slowly and talk about their concerns for that day. Optimists cheerfully eat what is in front of them, certain they will conquer whatever the new day offers.

Our early morning attitude sets the mood and the course for our day.

In my personal and professional life, I've been surprised that those who have the most reasons to be

A proud Army mother, Christina Neuharth, with son Walter, left, then a private, and son Al, then a corporal, both home on leave from overseas service in World War II.

pessimistic often are the most optimistic. Especially women and minorities.

Depression-age discrimination

My widowed mother was the first woman I saw being discriminated against. During the Depression of the '30s in South Dakota, she struggled to earn $10 a week washing dishes at a cafe and taking in laundry at home.

Meanwhile, men were earning $5 a day under President Franklin Delano Roosevelt's WPA (Works Progress Administration) often just by leaning on shovels. The very few women who got WPA jobs were paid $3 a day.

Under her circumstances, and considering the discrimination against her as a struggling single mother, my mom had many reasons to be a pessimist or become cynical. But she was nearly always cheerful and always encouraged my older brother, Walter, and me.

She constantly told us not to "worry." She firmly believed that there was light at the end of the tunnel. That same attitude rubbed off on her kids, because our childhood makes us what we are.

Those childhood memories made me determined as an adult to work for equal treatment, equal pay and equal opportunity for people of every age, race, sex and religion. Examples:

- ◆ At USA TODAY, we insisted that our leadership must reflect our readership. Our hiring practices put 51 percent women and 24 percent minorities in our newsroom.

- ◆ At The Freedom Forum, encouraging and sponsoring greater diversity in the nation's newspaper newsrooms became one of our top multimillion-dollar missions. We practiced what we preached. The Freedom Forum staff is over 30 percent minorities.

Cynics say those efforts at equality never will work.

Skeptics suggest that we're expecting too much fairness too fast.

Optimists know that equality and fairness will prevail. They are determined to dig to find the light at the end of the tunnel and get there as soon as possible.

 PLAIN TALK

Free spirits
see the
glass
half full,
not half
empty.

Oprah Winfrey

When I was promoting my 1989 best seller, "Confessions of an S.O.B.," Oprah Winfrey invited me to appear on her television show. On two conditions: that both of my ex-wives would be on, too. Each had written a chapter somewhat critical of me. Oprah insisted that they be seen and heard. A brilliant stroke that was a huge hit with her audience.

The Associated Press/Ed Bailey

Oprah Winfrey ballyhoos the premiere issue of *O* magazine in April 2000.

When my son Dan's book about overly controlling parents — me included — was published in 1998, Oprah had us both on. She said she admired me for showing up to face the criticism, but she agreed with Dan more often than she did with me.

Oprah is the queen of optimism and fair play. Her goal, "How do you get better?" inspires. Her new magazine, *O*, is helping millions of people see their glass as half full.

Larry King with his trademark suspenders and loud tie.

Larry King

Larry King sometimes gets knocked by critics for too many softball questions on CNN's "Larry King Live."

Every time I've been in front of Larry's microphone over the years, on radio and on the tube, I've come away upbeat. He allows his guests, as well as himself, to enjoy the experience.

Larry has had many personal and professional setbacks that might have changed his rose-colored glasses to dark-colored ones. Got fired from his first radio talk show in Miami. Has had one heart attack and one bypass surgery. But now, at age 66, is in his fifth marriage and has fathered two babies: Chance, age 20 months, and Cannon, age 6 months.

His optimistic outlook has remained as firm as his legendary suspenders.

CHAPTER 5

HOW TO HONK YOUR OWN HORN

*The greatest risk of all is the
risk of going unnoticed.* **"**

— Bill Bernbach

Once upon a time, if you built a better mousetrap, the world really would beat a path to your door. Not any more.

There are so many new "mousetraps" now. Hawked all over the world. Thanks especially to the Internet.

International barriers to new products or new ideas are down. That means an even greater opportunity to get attention for yourself or your product. Also, an even bigger risk of going unnoticed in a more crowded field.

CNN and Ted Turner quickly set the global news agenda after the satellite beamed that signal around the world in 1980. Bill Gates and his Microsoft led the way to one-on-one communications worldwide in 1985.

Honking loudly, or softly

Turner and Gates are among the world's best horn-honkers. Turner often a little too loudly. Gates

FREE SPIRIT

Fidel Castro, globe in hand, emphasizes a point about his place in the world during a six-hour nocturnal "debate" with Neuharth.

sometimes too softly.

Ideas are harder to promote than products or personalities.

When our Freedom Forum adopted the credo "Free Press. Free Speech. Free Spirit." we knew we had to do more than just preach it to the choir in the USA. We decided to go international, to places behind the "red curtain," where the sell was harder, but the need greater.

My first face-to-face meeting with a communist leader was with Cuba's Fidel Castro. We sparred for six hours, from 10 p.m. to 4 a.m.

Needless to say, my "free press" pitch got nowhere with him. But afterward, Fidel displayed

Charles L. Overby takes The Freedom Forum message to Moscow's Red Square on May Day, 1992.

his version of "free spirit" by inviting me to shoot baskets with him on his private basketball court.

After our Cuba foray, Christine Wells, our international senior vice president, decided to try to crack the two big reds in this order:

◆ The Soviet Union

◆ China

Wells arranged for meetings of our trustees and senior executives in Moscow in August 1991. We were there during the attempted coup against Premier Mikhail Gorbachev, when Boris Yeltsin climbed aboard a Red army tank to turn the hard-liners away.

As a result, The Freedom Forum established contacts that have made the foundation one of the most welcome disciples of the Western world in Russia.

In 1992, Freedom Forum President Charles L. Overby honked our horn before thousands in Red Square under a huge blue-and-white banner that read: Freedom Works!

China has been a tougher sell. But by late 1992, Wells convinced Beijing to let us hold media meetings there.

A language barrier

During my keynote address at a session in 1998, a very good translator turned my English into Mandarin. Had no problem with our credo of free press and free speech. But when I came to "free spirit," he hesitated.

"I'm sorry, those words are not in our vocabulary," he apologized.

International journalists among the hundreds present at the meeting picked up on that. They helped honk our horn recounting the "free spirit" episode.

After China had regained control of Hong Kong in July 1997, we held media forums there amid some concern that Beijing would stifle Hong Kong's free voices.

Jimmy Lai, brash and brilliant founder and publisher of the anti-Communist *Apple Daily* newspaper, reassured everyone:

Apple Daily Publisher Jimmy Lai at a Freedom Forum event in Hong Kong.

"Beijing has promised 'one country, two systems.' A few years from now it will be 'one country, one system.' Freedom will win."

The risk in honking your own horn is that you might honk it too loudly. When we started USA TODAY, I constantly warned our hucksters that "our promotion must be in step with our product, but not outrun it."

Don't spit in their eyes

Honking your horn personally is more difficult than doing it for a product or an idea. Some of us get carried away with our own importance.

I've made that mistake frequently. Instead of looking members of the establishment in the eye and saying "no" to their status quo, I sometimes spit in their eyes.

The former can get you respect, sometimes even

cooperation, albeit grudgingly. The latter generally stiffens the enemy's opposition.

Before you can honk your own horn effectively, you must bring attention to yourself. Nobody listens much to someone who is unknown.

Attention-getting can be anything from the way you dress to the way you talk.

When I was boss of Gannett, trying to put that company on the map, I wore only black-and-white clothing on my national and world travels. That became a readily recognized and sometimes ridiculed trademark. But it got me and Gannett noticed.

Talking tough with the guys

When Kay Graham first took over *The Washington Post* at her husband's death, she had to overcome her lack of professional experience and gain respect from the guys who then ran all other media companies.

She did it in part by talking tough language with them. Soon, she was welcomed into their dens.

She confronted her insecurities head-on. Overcoming her shyness, she even helped her autobiography, "Personal History," become a best seller by making hundreds of effective public appearances.

If you err in your horn honking, do it at the risk of a little too much flamboyancy rather than being deadly dull.

PLAIN TALK

Free spirits
know that
standing
quietly in line
doesn't get you
to the head of
the line.

Muhammad Ali

When he called himself "The Greatest," Muhammad Ali was seen by a lot of people as just another big braggart. Actually, he blew his horn pretty loudly when he was still known as Cassius Clay.

Muhammad Ali (then Cassius Clay) shouts "I am the greatest" after a 1964 championship fight.

"Float like a butterfly. Sting like a bee." "The thrilla in Manila." Ali's often-lyrical press agentry made for entertaining self-promotion. But he always understood that he had to deliver. That's why the world believes he was – and still is – the greatest.

When he was my guest on the Gannett jet flying from the "roast" of a mutual friend in Nashville to his training camp in Pennsylvania, he dazzled and charmed us with his non-stop mix of wit and wisdom.

A cocky guy with quick fists, a fast shuffle, a keen mind and a loud mouth.

Donald Trump tests the waters in 1999 for a presidential run.

The Associated Press/Chris Gardner

Donald Trump

When I first met Donald Trump at a Yankees game in George Steinbrenner's suite, we made small bets on hits and runs.

Later, I introduced him to Marty Birmingham, a banker and Freedom Forum trustee. That was after Trump almost went bust in real estate, leaving some creditors hanging. I told Trump that Birmingham was a former regional chairman of Marine Midland Bank.

Trump didn't miss a beat. "I think you're one of those that I paid back," he quipped.

Call it cockiness or confidence. That – and his consummate skill as a self-promoter – makes him known the world over as simply "The Donald."

CHAPTER 6

HOW TO FESS UP WHEN YOU MESS UP

An error becomes a mistake

when we refuse to admit it."

— Marilyn Vos Savant, 1987

The "cover-up" really is always more damaging than the "crime." At any age. In your personal or professional life.

Examples:

◆ Kids who lie to their parents about mischief or misdeeds generally lose more privileges or get more punishment than if they tell the truth.

◆ Grown-ups who deny their failures, or blame them on someone else, lose the respect of their friends or followers.

Failure is not fatal if you fess up. It can be more helpful to you than an uninterrupted string of successes. Especially if you fail when you're old enough to learn something from it, yet young enough to pick yourself up, dust yourself off and start over.

I experienced my first big failure at the perfect

Front page of first issue of Neuharth's ill-fated *SoDak Sports,* November 21, 1952.

Gannett Co., Inc.

age for failing: 29.

A college pal, Bill Porter, and I started a weekly newspaper called *SoDak Sports.* We had run the campus at the University of South Dakota, he as student body president and I as editor of *The Volante,* the student newspaper.

We thought *SoDak Sports,* printed on peach-colored newsprint to get special attention, would make us rich and famous. Begged and borrowed $50,000 to start it. Within two years, we went broke.

My first entrepreneurial venture failed because of mismanagement. I had mismanaged it.

A 30-year-old runaway

I was so embarrassed I ran away from home at age 30. Went all the way to Florida. Got a job as a reporter at *The Miami Herald.*

But I got that job because I didn't lie about my

failure. George Beebe, the managing editor of the *Herald*, told me the main reason he hired me was because I had openly acknowledged my South Dakota mistakes, and he thought I probably had learned a lot from them.

Ever since, I have not hesitated to accept the blame when things I'm involved in go wrong.

Just to make sure I don't forget how I screwed up back then, I have this constant reminder: All my many daily memos to others are on peach paper, a la *SoDak Sports*, pounded out on an old Royal typewriter like the one I used then.

That personal experience at failing has made me very critical of people who lie about their mistakes. Especially those who are prominent or in public office. The two best (or worst) examples:

◆ President Richard Milhous Nixon, a Republican.

◆ President William Jefferson Clinton, a Democrat.

Nixon had been a close friend of my predecessor as boss of the Gannett Company, Paul Miller. In some private conversations over drinks, I actually almost got to like Nixon. But when he lied repeatedly about Watergate, I crossed him off my list.

Clinton caught my eye when he was governor of Arkansas. After a meeting with him in the governor's mansion, I put him at the top of my published list of five most likely future presidents. But when he lied repeatedly about "Monicagate," I gave up on him.

Making embarrassing mistakes, personally or professionally, is a normal part of the wonderful, but risky, game of life.

Admitting them helps make us winners. Denying them makes us sure losers.

 PLAIN TALK

Free spirits
realize life
is not an
undefeated
season.

Bobby Knight

Bobby Knight was running pre-game drills for an Ohio State-Indiana basketball game. I was introduced to him and joked about the courtside chairs being chained to the floor. "Whose idea was that?" I asked. "Mine, to help keep myself under control," he said, laughing.

Coach Bobby Knight at his infamous chair-throwing in 1985.

The Associated Press

Knight is an NCAA Hall of Fame coach, a very spirited and basically pretty nice guy. But his old-fashioned, drill-sergeant discipline on and off the court doesn't work anymore. In my USA TODAY "Plain Talk" column, written long before the incident that triggered Knight's firing, I said he should quit because he had lost his touch.

His touch was too heavy-handed.

Knight never fully admitted, even to himself, the extent of his bullying. Had he faced up to his problem, he might have reformed, and he might still be at his beloved Indiana.

Bill Clinton

The Associated Press/Greg Gibson

"I did not have sexual relations with that woman," President Clinton tells a TV audience.

I grasped Bill Clinton's political skill and personal charm when I interviewed all 50 governors in 1987. It was part of the BusCapade promotion for USA TODAY. The gang on board talked frequently about who we thought were rising stars.

Among Democratic governors, Clinton topped the list. He wowed us. Then I called him in print: Brilliant. Brainy. Polished.

Now I call him President Pinocchio.

He's a free spirit in many ways. That has led him to many highs and lows in his personal and political life. But he never learned how to fess up when he messed up.

CHAPTER 7

HOW TO HAVE FUN ON THE JOB

Laugh and the world laughs with you;

Weep, and you weep alone. **"**

— Ella Wheeler Wilcox, 1883

There's an old axiom that you shouldn't mix business with pleasure. Wrong. We should have as much fun on the job as we have at home or at play.

All work and no play really do make Jack and Jane dull boys and girls. Also, their parents.

I've had more fun on the job during the latest 20 years of my life than in the previous 55. That's because I belatedly realized that business and pleasure both benefit when you mix them. Examples:

- ◆ BusCapade, a 50-state, six-month tour over 35,905 miles of highways and byways in 1987 to tout USA TODAY, then just 5 years old and a huge hit with readers but still struggling to get the advertising to make it consistently profitable.

- ◆ JetCapade, a six-continent fly around in 1988 to prepare for the launching of USA TODAY International. We covered 148,261 miles in seven months and interviewed 32 heads of state.
- ◆ TrainCapade, a 38-state, 16,000-mile, six-week rail ride in 1995 to call attention to The Freedom Forum and its programs fostering free press, free speech and free spirit.
- ◆ NewsCapade, an 18-month, 50-state road show in 1999 and 2000 to promote The Freedom Forum's Newseum, the world's only interactive museum of news.

In each case, the promotion could have been handled in more conventional ways, like newspaper or TV ads. But that would not have been any fun for me and co-workers and probably not as productive long term.

Not just the tours, but their titles were important in the business/pleasure mix.

Deadly dull doesn't work

When we planned BusCapade, some of my associates feared we would not be taken seriously with that title. They favored something dull, like "On the

An unshaven and relaxed Neuharth enjoys a break during a seven-day bus trip on the "Alcan" Highway to Alaska during NewsCapade in 2000.

Jack Marsh

Road" or "Seeing the USA by Bus."

When we planned NewsCapade, there was similar resistance to the "frivolous" title. Some wanted to call it "Newseum on Wheels" or "Newseum on the Road."

These escapades, by any other name, would have been far less fun and far less productive.

What you call what you do is important, in business or pleasure. "Brand" names sell ideas or products.

The most important thing is that you have

fun. That will be reflected in your relationship with others.

Kids should have fun in school. Grown-ups should have fun at work. Astronauts should have fun in space or on the moon.

PLAIN TALK

Free spirits
take the
world
seriously but
don't take
themselves
too seriously.

Alan Shepard

Alan B. Shepard Jr. was the first American in space and one of just 12 people to walk on the moon. I met him when he and the other original Mercury astronauts were "in training" but also having fun on the beaches and in the bars at Cocoa Beach, Florida.

Alan B. Shepard Jr. interrupts his moon walk to hit a golf ball for a "crater-in-one."

Later, he took a microfilmed copy of our FLORIDA TODAY newspaper to the moon with him. He also smuggled two golf balls and a six iron aboard Apollo 14. A worldwide TV audience laughed and shared his thrill when he hit a golf ball that carried for miles. He called it a "crater-in-one."

When he retired from NASA, he joined our Freedom Forum Board of Trustees. He inspired people at our forums around the world with his fun-loving spirit, just as he had on the moon.

Lillian Carter signs autographs on her porch in Plains, Georgia.

Lillian Carter

Lillian Carter, or "Miss Lillian" as she was known, was the mother of Jimmy Carter who during the 1976 presidential campaign promised he would "never lie."

I met her at her modest home in Plains, Georgia. Earlier she had received a reporter there who had pressed her about her son's "never lie" pledge.

Miss Lillian explained to the female reporter the difference between a "real lie" and a "little white lie."

"It's like when I met you at the door and told you how nice you looked and how glad I was to see you," she said, smiling sweetly.

Miss Lillian, who joined the Peace Corps at age 67 and served two years in India, took the world seriously but never took herself too seriously.

CHAPTER 8

HOW TO AVOID THE "AWKWARD AGE" SYNDROME

> **"** *Age is mind over matter. If you*
> *don't mind, it doesn't matter.* **"**
>
> — Leroy "Satchel" Paige, 1982

Most people dread or fear "old age," even though we differ on how to define it.

Many men and women worry about approaching 50. The big Five-Oh scares some for years in advance.

Some younger people also fear earlier signposts, like 30 or 40.

Ten-year-olds often worry about becoming a teen.

Kids sometimes are scared of age 6 and having to go to school.

I've lived through all those milestones. But they really weren't put in perspective for me until my 75th birthday.

Some of my friends and co-workers organized a big bash for that occasion — a roast and toast.

Among the roasters was the minority leader of

Daughter Alexis, then 8, ribs her dad about USA TODAY's lack of comics during Neuharth's 75th birthday roast. USA TODAY Publisher Tom Curley enjoys her joshing.

the U.S. Senate, Democrat Tom Daschle, a fellow South Dakotan. Daschle got the biggest laugh of the evening with these lines:

"Seventy-five is an awkward age for a journalist — too old to run a major newspaper and too young to work on '60 Minutes.' "

Daschle drove home this point: Some of us mistakenly think we're either too young or too old for certain of life's adventures.

At the same roast, the youngest to take the mike was our then 8-year-old, first-adopted daughter, Alexis.

Facing 270 adult VIP guests and a live national

TV audience on C-SPAN2, Alexis opened with this kids' quip:

"Wow! I've never been in a room with so many really old people!"

Alexis concluded with this dig at her dad:

"He'll probably tell you he's going to invent something new again. Some of the things he invents are pretty good, but some are not.

"Like USA TODAY. I don't think that's such a great newspaper. It doesn't even have any comics in it."

Daschle and Alexis both demonstrated that people of any age can have fun with those who are at their so-called "awkward age."

Fact is, of course, there is no such thing as an awkward age. Rather, every stage of our life presents awesome opportunities.

These are my suggested seasons for all ages:

- In your pre-teens, play all you can.
- In your teens, mix a little work with play.
- In your 20s, put learning ahead of earning.
- In your 30s, rate risks above rules and routine.
- In your 40s, earn all you can.
- In your 50s, invest all you can to secure your future financially.
- In your 60s, immunize yourself against "hangonitis" on the job.

- In your 70s and thereafter, enjoy all the old and new adventures you can.

We're never too young or too old to get the most out of life.

 **PLAIN TALK**

Free spirits
challenge
themselves
at any age.

Tom Brokaw

Tom Brokaw wrote a long piece 10 years ago for *The New York Times* about turning 50. He likened it to "a chronic, low-level virus."

This wasn't Tom's first "awkward" passage. In his early 20s at the University of South Dakota — the alma mater for both of us — Tom majored in beer-drinking and carousing as a freshman and sophomore.

Tom Brokaw has been the sole anchor of "NBC Nightly News" since 1983.

Corbis Outline/Michael O'Neill

William O. "Doc" Farber, a savvy professor, suggested Tom take a semester off from school. He did. Came back, settled down a bit, studied a little and earned a degree in political science.

Tom got over the transitional anguish of turning 20 and of facing the big Five-Oh. "Now," he says, "60 doesn't seem old to me anymore."

Helen Thomas, in her 57th year as a reporter, at the 2000 Republican National Convention.

The Associated Press/Eddie Adams

Helen Thomas

To many, Helen Thomas always will be the dean of White House correspondents. We first met in the late '50s when we both were in the Washington press corps.

It took determination to report on the presidency for more than 40 years. But it took spirit for a woman to rise from a $17.50-a-week copy girl to become the first female member — and later president — of the stuffy Gridiron Club.

She has filled her life with milestones — not charted by passing years but by achievement. Not an awkward moment among them. Now 80, she is cherished by a nation as a gracious but gutsy lady who ended hundreds of press conferences by saying, "Thank you, Mr. President."

CHAPTER 9

HOW TO MIND YOUR BODY AND YOUR MIND

If you rest, you rust. "

— Helen Hayes, 1985

Most of us keep our mind working as long as we can. Many of us put our body to rest long before it's ready.

Eat too much. Drink too much. Smoke our way to becoming a premature skeleton.

Sit when we should be standing or stretching. Stroll when we could be scurrying.

I started smoking while I was in the Army at 19, because cigarettes came with our K-rations. Quit when I was 29.

Ate several ice creams every day when I worked as a soda jerk at Bentsen's drug store in Alpena, South Dakota, when I was 16. Have limited myself to one or two low-fat yogurts a week since I was 50.

Had salami or steak or hamburger every day when I worked as a butcher boy at age 14. Now, it's still red meat at least once a week, but usually selected and cooked properly by me, not at a greasy spoon.

One reason so many of us have trouble selecting and sticking to a healthful diet is that even the experts disagree.

The latest and lingering controversy involves two of the country's most popular diets.

- New York cardiologist Robert Atkins prescribes bacon and hamburgers. He says carbohydrates are the body's enemy.
- California internist Dean Ornish is a virtual vegetarian. He preaches strict low fat.

Mine is a mix of Atkins and Ornish. Meat and potatoes. But also lots of fruit and vegetables. And don't forget my vodka martini before dinner.

Keeping your body in shape means much more than just watching what you put into it. We must keep all the parts moving. Regularly.

Weekend golfing is not enough. Your heart and your muscles need a workout at least five days a week.

That's easier than you may think. These most useful exercises can be effectively completed in an hour or less:

- Jogging
- Swimming

♦ Speed walking

Golf is both time-consuming and thought-consuming. You can't think of anything really important while concentrating on a drive, pitch or putt.

Your mind can be put to work during individual exercises. Some of my best ideas have come to me when jogging, alone.

I started jogging at age 30. Still do it five days a week, although our 9-year-old Alexis says it's more like "an old man's shuffle."

Neuharth on his favorite jogging "trail," the beach in front of his Florida home.

Gannett Co., Inc.

Exercising the brain

Keeping your mind alert is even easier than keeping your body fit.

In my case, as a lifelong journalist, writing is a natural form of working the brain. Since my retirement from active management at USA TODAY, I have written more than 600 weekly columns.

Consecutively. Never missed a week.

That forces me to keep up on everything from Wall Street to world affairs, sports to space shuttle launches, food and fashion, politics and other entertainment.

Reading. Writing. Discussing. Debating. Nearly all of us can engage in these mental exercises from pre-school to post-retirement.

Alertness over dullness and fitness over fatness both are mostly matters of mind over body.

PLAIN TALK

Free spirits
make regular
use of
all their parts.

Strom Thurmond

Whenever I get to feeling real good about myself as a 76-year-old, I think about Sen. Strom Thurmond. He was considered an "elder" statesman back in the '70s when we were introduced at a Gridiron Club dinner in Washington.

Sen. Strom Thurmond, at 96, presides over the Senate during the Clinton impeachment trial.

The Associated Press/APTN

Now 97. Still sharp-tongued, strong-spirited and perking right along. Strom is the vanguard of an era promising unimagined longevity and productivity for those who keep both their mind and body working.

The decorated World War II paratrooper has served in the Senate since 1954. Most of those years he jogged or walked to his Capitol Hill office. You might not embrace his South Carolina politics, but you've got to admire his endurance.

Nelson Mandela, sprightly in his 80s, dances for his fans.

Nelson Mandela

We hosted Nelson Mandela at The Freedom Forum in 1993. Soon afterward, he was elected president of the country that had jailed him for 27 years as a political prisoner. I was struck by his intellect. But even more by his great stamina and spirit.

He is proof that even after years of suffering, life can be full and fulfilling.

Mandela was 71 when released from prison. Seventy-six when elected president. Probably could have been re-elected president for life. But he remarried at 80 and stepped to the political sidelines.

As an elder statesman, strong as ever of body and mind, he continues to spread his belief that the Republic of South Africa belongs to all her people.

CHAPTER 10

HOW TO LEAD AND HOW TO LEAVE

Walk sober off before the sprightlier age ...

shoves you from the stage. **"**

— Alexander Pope, 1738

O̶ur educational system, from grade school to high school to college to graduate school, offers lessons on how to become a leader.

Hardly any schools offer practical advice on how and when to leave.

Results:

- ◆ Most businesses and professions have above-average to excellent leadership.
- ◆ "Hangonitis" is a serious sickness among stars or leaders in nearly every field.

Professional athletes, coaches or managers want just one more winning season. Corporate CEOs want just one more year of record profits. Politicians want to win just one more election. Entertainers want just one more Oscar or Emmy or curtain call.

Whether you're the boss or star of a family business,

a small private company, a Fortune 500 public corporation or a sports team, the most important aspect of your leadership is your preparation for leaving.

That means setting a firm timetable for your departure and training and naming possible successors.

Most people "retire" only once, so it's understandable why some mess it up. I've had two big-time "retirements." Waffled a bit on the first one but got the second one right.

When I was chairman and CEO of Gannett, the nation's largest newspaper company, I promised the board and myself I would retire from that post at age 65.

Looking for the best

When I was 57, I mistakenly concluded no executive inside Gannett was a strong candidate to become CEO. So I offered the chance to succeed me to Tom Johnson, then publisher of the *Los Angeles Times*, and the person I thought was the best all-around young newspaper executive in the country.

Cleared my choice of Johnson with key members of the Gannett board. The two senior members of the management continuity committee — former Associated Press General Manager Wes Gallagher and former NBC Chairman Julian Goodman — both lobbied Johnson to accept. We offered him a million-dollar annual compensation package, at a time when a million was still big money.

Johnson very seriously considered the offer from November 1981 to January 1982, then graciously declined because he thought the future at Times Mirror was much brighter than it turned out to be. Otis Chandler and family fouled that up. Johnson left and is now chairman of CNN.

When Johnson said no, I turned back inside Gannett to identify and train a successor. Ultimately selected John Curley, president of the Newspaper Division, to become chairman and CEO and Doug McCorkindale, chief financial officer, as president.

Chose Curley because I thought his news background would make him a visionary, free-spirited leader. Actually, McCorkindale, a first-class beancounter but with personal interests and talents ranging from piano playing to wrestling, may have more vision, free spirit, style and stamina.

Curley took early retirement in 2000. McCorkindale moved up to the well-deserved boss's role.

A second chance to choose

When the sun set on my Gannett career at age 65, as I had long planned, I rode off into another sunrise as chairman of the Gannett Foundation and helped transform it into what is now The Freedom Forum, a billion dollar-plus international nonprofit organization.

Eugene Dorsey, president of the foundation, was widely expected to become chairman. He was a gentleman. An avid golfer. Magnificent in front of a microphone. But he lacked vision.

So I convinced Charles L. Overby, longtime Gannett journalist and Pulitzer Prize-winning editor, to come aboard and become Freedom Forum president. Eight years later we named him chairman and I "retired" again.

Overby and his colleagues have made The Freedom Forum and its Newseum a well-respected foundation in the nation's capital and one of the most highly regarded nonprofits in the USA and the world.

Part-time work and fun

Many have asked me why I keep writing my weekly "Plain Talk" column in USA TODAY since my "retirement." Several reasons. It's a part-time, not full-time, job. It's fun. It keeps me in touch with people and them in touch with me, through feedback, phone calls and letters. It doesn't contradict my "when to lead and when to leave" philosophy because I retain no leadership role whatsoever at USA TODAY.

Writing, teaching and preaching may be three of the easiest professions for part-time work, including fun and satisfaction, at any advanced age.

Let me leave you with these thoughts about the personal side of retirement.

These three things are most important in your sunset years:

- ◆ Family
- ◆ Finances
- ◆ Fun

If you have children or grandchildren, give them the affection and attention that you sometimes denied them when you were scratching to meet the mortgage payments or climbing the career ladder.

Long before you're 50, put money aside and put it to work to grow for your golden years. Don't count on just your company or your country to put food on your table, keep a roof over your head or refill your medicine cabinet.

Far too many middle-aged men and women still think these are the keys to fun in retirement:

- ◆ A fishing pole
- ◆ Golf clubs
- ◆ A rocking chair

Nothing wrong with any or all of the above. But they're not enough. We need to use every ounce of our energy to enjoy new enterprises or new

FREE SPIRIT

escapades until the day we die.

Speaking of which, death really is as inevitable as taxes. So plan for it.

Most adults 50 or over now have a will of sorts. Those generally deal with how they want their possessions to be distributed. That should rule out family squabbles over material things.

But the burden on family members to arrange funeral or memorial services after a death can be agonizing and distressing.

Planning your farewell

My family and friends have been given written and videotaped instructions on how to celebrate our lives spent together after my demise.

Where. Who should be invited. What songs to sing. What verses to recite. What to drink and eat. How to laugh and love at the celebration.

Even a few parting words from me on how they should go on living the wonderful game of life until we meet again.

I hope all present will walk away smiling and saying, "What a way to go!"

 PLAIN TALK

Free spirits
know how
to enjoy
sunrises
and
sunsets.

Don Shula and Dan Marino

When NBC anchor Tom Brokaw couldn't accept NFL owner Joe Robbie's invitation to emcee the dedication of Robbie's new stadium outside Miami in 1987, our mutual South Dakota pal turned to me. Second fiddle usually isn't my cup of tea, but this was great fun. As a huge Dolphins fan, I got to hang out with some people I admired.

Among them: Dolphins Coach Don Shula and superstar quarterback Dan Marino. Ironically, they are two sports legends I would later criticize in my column for hanging on too long.

It's tough knowing when you've peaked. Even tougher coming to grips with the signs you're slipping. Both Shula and Marino saw the signs. Neither heeded them.

Though he had a year left on his contract, Shula was forced to quit in 1996. Dolphins fans had been screaming for his head for years.

Shula took teams to Super Bowls six times in 33 seasons. Won two, including one that capped an unprecedented undefeated season in 1972. But Shula hadn't been back to the big bowl for 12 years. His winning percentage had been on a steady decline.

Marino quarterbacked that last and losing Dolphins Super Bowl appearance. Despite a host of records, including career passing yards (61,361) and career touchdown passes (420),

The Associated Press/Rick Bowmer

Former Miami Dolphins Coach Don Shula and star quarterback Dan Marino hug after Marino breaks another passing record in 1995.

Marino, too, didn't know when the ballgame was over.

He hung on after a neck injury early in the '99 season. Threw for 12 more touchdowns, but misfired for 17 costly interceptions. Then was belatedly and rudely benched by the bosses.

Both Shula and Marino deservedly are legends in Miami and in the pro football world. But they would be happier in retirement if they had left the playing field before they were shoved off. Like so many leaders, they didn't know when to leave.

The making of millionaires and of journalists ...

Free spirit might make a millionaire out of you or someone you know. How and why:

As I approached my 75th birthday, Charles L. Overby, chairman and CEO of The Freedom Forum, told me that he and the 14 other trustees unanimously had agreed to rename the original, highly popular $50 million Newseum in Arlington, Virginia, after me.

On March 22, 1999, it would officially become the Neuharth Newseum, he said.

Had a nice ring to it! I was flattered. Then, on a morning jog, I really got to thinking about it.

The Newseum is not about its founder or any other individual, I realized. It's about the First Amendment freedoms. Especially about the courageous media people involved in free-spirited journalism.

A costly substitute

When the new name came up for a vote at the next trustees' meeting, I expressed my gratitude but declined for the reasons above. But I told the board I would be honored to accept some other, more appropriate recognition with my name on it. "Hopefully, a costly one," I quipped.

That's how the Al Neuharth Free Spirit of the Year Award came to be. The board set up a $25 million endowment. The Free Spirit recipient, recipients or designees will get up to $1 million at an annual award ceremony.

Nominations for the award can be made by anyone. All nominations will be considered by a Free Spirit Award Selection Committee. A winner or winners will be recommended to The Freedom Forum Board of Trustees for final approval.

Nominations may be sent to:

Al Neuharth Free Spirit Award
The Freedom Forum
1101 Wilson Boulevard
Arlington, VA 22209
USA

Free-spirited student journalists

The $25 million endowment also funds an annual Al Neuharth Free Spirit Scholarship and Conference program.

The program awards $1,000 college scholarships to outstanding high school students who are interested in pursuing journalism careers and who demonstrate qualities of free spirit.

The Freedom Forum works with newspapers across the USA to solicit applications from high school seniors. They must submit samples of their journalistic work and write an essay on free spirit. The scholarship winners are chosen through a competitive process.

Two winning students from each of the 50 states and the District of Columbia are selected. The winners participate in a three-day journalism conference in Washington at Freedom Forum expense.

A list of the students and the participating newspapers is available on the Web at freedomforum.org/freespirit.

ACKNOWLEDGMENTS

The making of this book ...

After my autobiography, "Confessions of an S.O.B.," had its run on the best-seller lists and after publisher Doubleday made me run around the country promoting it, I vowed I'd never write another book. That was 1989.

Ten years later, my associates at The Freedom Forum, many of them earlier co-workers with me at Gannett and USA TODAY, changed my mind. They convinced me I should tell you about some of the interesting and rewarding things we've been up to over the past 10 years. Also give you a new glimpse at some earlier stuff that might help you.

These people deserve the credit – or the blame – for this book:

- ◆ Charles L. Overby, chairman and CEO of The Freedom Forum, and Peter S. Prichard, president. They turned loose their staff to help me in preparing the book. Equally important, they paid for the printing!

- ◆ John C. Quinn. He was the conscience of the Gannett Company and is elder statesman of The Freedom Forum. Always good for short bursts of facts, sometimes mixed with a little delightful baffle and b.s.

- Rod Sandeen. Handles administration for Overby and company. His low-key, high-result style was most responsible for putting this book in your hands.
- J. Taylor Buckley and Sharon Shahid. They spent months researching and reporting on the highlights of these "how tos."
- Patty Casey, whose artistic and creative talent resulted in all the eye-pleasing design and layout.

Many, many more. If I gave them all the paragraph they deserve, this segment would be longer than any chapter in the book.

So let me list them alphabetically and thank them all most gratefully: Gordon Aadland, Jerrie Bethel, Janet Daniels, Yvonne Egertson, Juanie Fuqua, Pam Galloway-Tabb, Suzette Karelis, Jack Marsh, Ken Paulson, Don Ross, John Seigenthaler, Nancy Stewart, Joe Urschel, Chris Wells, Karen Wyatt.

BOOK ORDER FORM

"Free Spirit" was published by The Freedom Forum's Newseum. It is not available in bookstores, but can be purchased at the Newseum Store in Arlington, Virginia.

To order by mail, use the form below.

* * *

Ship to:

Name: _____

Address: _____

City: _____

State: _____Zip Code: _____

Telephone: _____

Please send me _____ copy(ies) of Al Neuharth's "Free Spirit." ($9.95 each including handling charges for one to four books. $8.95 each in quantities of five or more. $7.95 each in quantities of 20 or more.)

Make check or money order payable to the Newseum and mail to:
    Free Spirit
    Newseum Store
    1101 Wilson Boulevard
    Arlington, Virginia 22209

Or order online at www.newseum.org.